I WAS THERE

Ira Aldridge
The Shakespearean Actor

Judy Hepburn

■SCHOLASTIC

Published in the UK by Scholastic Children's Books, 2021
Euston House, 24 Eversholt Street, London, NW1 1DB
A division of Scholastic Limited

London ~ New York ~ Toronto ~ Sydney ~ Auckland
Mexico City ~ New Delhi ~ Hong Kong

ISBN 978 0702 30496 5

A CIP catalogue record for this book is available from the British Library.

Printed and bound by CPI Group (UK) Ltd, Croydon, CR0 4YY
Papers used by Scholastic Children's Books are made
from wood grown in sustainable forests.

2 4 6 8 10 9 7 5 3 1

While this book is based on real characters and actual historical events,
some situations and people are fictional, created by the author.

www.scholastic.co.uk

CHAPTER ONE

Hello. My name is Fred Jonas and I'm going to be ten years old on 14 October 1833. So that makes me nine and a half. To be honest, I'm not sure what day I was born, but everyone has to have a birthday, don't they?

At the moment I'm lying in my cosy corner, covered with blankets. There's a nice warm spot at my feet, which means that Trooper, the theatre cat and my best friend, is curled up fast asleep. I can hear him purring. He must be having a nice dream.

A curtain separates me from the rest of the room and a patch of light on my blankets tells me the sun is rising and London is waking up.

Way down below in the street, I can hear the slow clip-clopping of an old horse. It stops – there is a faraway sound of voices and a scrape of something heavy being moved. Then I hear a rumble. I thought so. It's the coal delivery, rattling down into the cellar.

Coal fires are wonderful. They last longer than wood fires. The only thing is that coal has to be dug out of the earth.

I wouldn't want that job. It's dangerous in the underground pits, especially for children, as you have to work in the smallest spaces where the grown-ups can't reach. My job is much safer.

Although I am only nine, I have to go to work. I am the call boy and a stagehand in one of the oldest and best theatres in London, the Theatre Royal in Covent Garden. It's a very busy theatre so I am always rushing around.

Mr Simpkin runs the theatre and he is my boss. He gives me a lot of jobs to do, like checking the actors are on time for their performance and keeping the theatre clean and tidy.

When Mr Simpkin is in a good mood, he likes to tell me about all the new inventions he reads about in his newspaper. Like the steam engine, for instance,

that's his favourite at the moment.

Let me see if I can remember. George Stephenson, an engineer, uses coal to boil water. Boiling water makes steam and pushing steam into pipes makes energy. George Stephenson's steam engines pull and push carts full of coal. They pull more than horses ever can.

Now these steam engines are carrying people too, from city to city, all around the country. Mr Simpkin says that very soon there are going to be steamships as well, which will travel faster than sailing boats.

I love my job, but there are so many new inventions and exciting things happening these days I might do anything when I grow up.

Maybe I'll become a sailor, even though I've never seen the sea. I've never left London, in fact. All I know is the backstage of the theatre, with its dressing rooms and winding staircase, but every time the Theatre Royal puts on a different play I travel to a new place in the world. I walk along the streets of Venice, sit on a throne or get shipwrecked. This is because the painted scenery is so real. I suppose you could say daydreaming is my hobby.

Shall I tell you a secret? I would like to become the manager of a theatre. It's only a dream, but how nice it would be to sell tickets in the box office, or decide what plays to put on, or count the money at the end of an evening, all dressed up in my best clothes.

I need to get up soon, but it's so warm under the blankets I close my eyes again. The patch of sunlight and the sounds and the faraway voices outside keep me from falling asleep again.

The Theatre Royal. The name alone thrills me. I have seen the King and Queen seated in the royal box. I expected the King to be wearing a crown but he wasn't. The Queen was though, a small one that glittered when she moved her head.

She is much younger than the King. They say she is a kind and generous woman who makes the King do kind and generous things that he doesn't really want to do. For instance, the Queen thinks all children should be able to read and write and that all slaves should be set free.

Both of these things are important to me. I want to learn to read and write and I don't ever want to be a slave, or want anyone else to be a slave.

Now, you ask, how do I know these things about the King and Queen? Well, I know about them from Mrs Booth of course!

Mrs Booth works in the wardrobe department, making costumes for the theatre. She keeps all the outfits clean and she always smells like summer flowers. Her eyes are watery, her orange curls are turning grey and she hasn't got many teeth left, but when she laughs her eyes shine and she wobbles all over. I love her very much. She looks out for me and always makes sure I have something to eat.

You see, I don't have any parents. I don't even remember them. But please don't feel sorry for me. I have somewhere warm to sleep and Mrs Booth is like family to me, so I am lucky.

I love the wardrobe department. It's one of the only places backstage with windows – the sunlight floods in on bright days and warms it up. The room needs to be light because you need to be able to see well to

stitch and lots of stitching goes on in there.

Then there are the costumes, racks of beautiful clothes made of silk and satin and velvet and lace. I never get to wear any of them because all the stagehands have to dress in black so the audience can't see us as we move about backstage.

You see, everyone has a role to play in the running of the theatre, even Trooper!

All theatres have a cat because theatres have mice and cats catch mice for their dinner – that's Trooper's job. His skinny tail sticks up behind him and sways from side to side when he walks. Wherever I am, Trooper is never far away. I can't imagine life without him.

One of my jobs is to sweep the stage every day with a very large broom. If I lie down beside it the broom is almost as long as me. I know because I tried it out one day. I can feel the bristles now, tickling my face…

Wait a minute! Those tickles are real! I open my eyes and discover Trooper staring at me, his whiskers tickling my cheeks. I think he's trying to say, "Wake up! I'm hungry! It's time for breakfast."

I reach out and stroke the back of his head, then give him a scratch behind the ears.

He stretches his neck to one side showing me where he wants to be scratched next. I give that spot a rub.

"*Miaow*."

"Okay, Trooper, you're right, I need to get up. It's time to go to work."

I get up, pull the curtain to one side and open a cupboard. I take out a jug of milk, a chunk of bread and some fried herrings that Mrs Booth put in there last night before she went home.

I pour out a saucer of milk for Trooper and watch him lap it up while I munch on the bread and fish and get myself ready for the day.

CHAPTER TWO

It's evening now and we've got to be quiet because I'm backstage in the middle of a performance. We can't even whisper.

I have to stand by Mr Simpkin during

the show and follow his orders. I don't mind because I get to watch the actors. Who knows, I might be an actor one day!

We get lots of different shows at the theatre. The one that's playing at the moment is called *Othello*. It's about a man with dark skin, like me, who is a big fancy army officer. It's very sad because Othello's best friend, Iago, is jealous of him and tells lies about Othello's wife, Desdemona. Othello believes the lies, gets very angry and upset and kills Desdemona. Then he feels very sad and he takes his own life. I don't really like the ending but William Shakespeare, who wrote it, is England's most famous writer and everyone else seems to like it – they even clap at the end.

Most of *Othello* happens at a seaport in Cyprus but the story starts off in Venice, an old city in Italy, with beautifully carved stone buildings and streets made of water. People have to travel in boats instead of in carriages.

But hush, I'm listening for my cue. (That means when it's my turn to do something.) It's coming up soon. I love this bit. It's near the beginning when Desdemona's father discovers she has married Othello without telling him. As soon as her father raises his arm and says:

"Look to her, Moor, if thou hast eyes to see: She has deceived her father, and may thee."

Mr Simpkin told me that a "Moor" is what people call Othello sometimes because of the colour of his skin. I'm not sure where Othello is from, some people think it's Africa, but I like that he's different from a lot of other characters in the plays that I have seen. He is a good man, I think, and treated unfairly.

When I hear the actor say those words in the play, that's when I shake a sheet of metal hard. It makes a noise like thunder!

Everyone calls me Fred, except for Mr Simpkin. He always calls me Frederick.

"Frederick, fetch my list. Frederick, sweep the stage. Frederick, go and buy my lunch."

I have to do whatever he asks. He isn't unkind, but he isn't very friendly either.

Sometimes I imagine what it would be like to be an important actor so I could tell Mr Simpkin what to do. "Mr Simpkin, bring me my lunch, fetch my costume, find my sword," I would say.

Actually, his first name is Peter so I would probably say, "Peter, bring me my lunch." Yes, that sounds better. "Peter, fetch me my sword. Peter—"

"Frederick! You are daydreaming again.

Listen up!"

"Yes, Mr Simpkin."

He always catches me daydreaming and tells me off. I make sure I'm holding the sheet of metal properly and start paying attention.

Mr Kean, who is playing Othello, is striding about the stage, looking important and talking loudly. He's very good and the audience love him.

Wait a minute, what's happening? Mr Kean is speaking but his voice is sounding funny and he's staggering. He's not supposed to stagger. He's playing a big, strong general in command of his troops. I look up at Mr Simpkin. His eyes are very wide. Suddenly, Mr Kean falls over and lies on the stage, completely still. Everyone is very shocked.

"Lower the curtain," Mr Simpkin hisses.

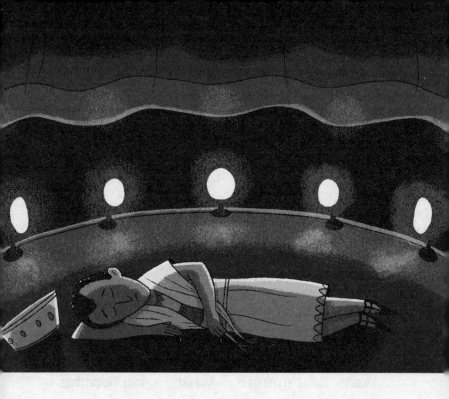

I put the sheet of metal on the floor and run over to help pull the ropes that drop the curtain in between the stage and the audience.

Once the curtain is down Mr Simpkin hurries on to the stage and bends over Mr Kean.

"Frederick, run and fetch the doctor for Mr Kean. Be quick!"

I don't wait to hear any more. I know where the doctor lives. Every theatre is supposed to have a doctor on call in case of emergencies just like this. Our doctor lives around the corner for this very reason. I find him sitting at the dining table, eating his supper.

He gets up straight away and grabs his medicine bag, which is always packed and ready. Very soon we're back in Mr Kean's dressing room. The actor is lying on his couch. He sits up when we come in but he looks sick. It doesn't help that the black make-up on his face has gone streaky. I want to laugh but everyone looks very serious, so I don't. It isn't appropriate. Mrs Booth is cleaning his face and Mr Kean now looks very pale indeed.

"Mr Kean cannot continue," the doctor says. "He needs complete rest. I am afraid

you will have to cancel all future shows."

Mr Simpkin frowns. "I can't do that," he says. "I'll have to return a lot of money. We shall all lose our jobs!"

"You don't understand, Mr Simpkin. There is no choice in the matter. Mr Kean is far too ill to continue."

CHAPTER THREE

I didn't sleep a wink last night. I couldn't stop worrying about what will happen now that Mr Kean is too unwell to play Othello.

Supposing the theatre does close and we all lose our jobs? What will happen to me? I'll have to go and live on the streets and sell matches or something. Either that or go into the workhouse and get sent miles away to Lancashire or somewhere, where kids have to do all the dangerous work in the cotton mills. I don't fancy that at all. Or I might even have to go to Newcastle and dig the coal out from underground.

It's times like these I wish I had someone

to comfort me. Even though Trooper snuggled up with me last night when I was crying, I still pulled out my mother's cream-coloured handkerchief from under my pillow and cuddled into its softness. I often pretend it's her dress I'm cuddling into and my blanket is her arms but last night it didn't work.

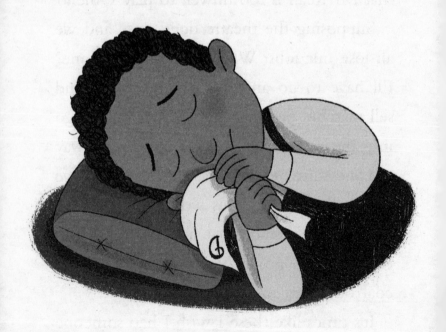

Dark pink roses go around the edge of the handkerchief and a garland of green leaves joins the roses together. There's a pink initial, "D", embroidered in a corner. Her name was Dorothea but everyone called her Dora, Mrs Booth says. I like to think my mother embroidered all those roses and leaves herself. It's the only thing I have of hers and it's my treasure. I have it with me always. It's in my pocket now, all crumpled and tear-stained from last night.

All of us, cast and crew, are assembled on the stage. It's morning and Mr Simpkin is going to address us. We are standing about with long faces, and some people are whispering to each other. There is none of the usual joking. Mr Simpkin clears his throat and everyone stops to look at him. Are we all about to lose our jobs?

"As you know, our leading actor, Mr Kean, was taken ill last night and cannot continue in his role as Othello. We wish him well. We were gravely concerned that the show would have to close and the theatre go dark but I am pleased to say that another actor is ready, able and willing to step into his shoes. We open tomorrow evening."

Mr Simpkin stops and looks at one of the actors stood next to him.

"We have Charles to thank for this stroke of luck."

Charles is Mr Kean's son and he is playing Iago in our production. Everyone starts clapping and Charles makes a bow to accept the applause.

"Charles is a friend of our new leading man and asked him last night if he would accept the challenge. He did. Our new Othello will be none other than the famous

African Roscius, Ira Aldridge."

A gasp goes around the stage and everyone starts talking at once.

"But he can't learn all those lines in a single day!" one of the stagehands says.

"He's played the part many times before," Charles replies. "And we'll be making history for the Theatre Royal."

Mr Simpkin raises his hand and all the chattering stops.

"Yes, you are right. We shall be making history. It will be the first time in our theatre that a black man will play the part of Othello. What is the date today, Frederick?"

Mr Simpkin likes to put me on the spot so I try to prepare myself for anything.

"Today is the ninth of April 1833, Mr Simpkin," I say.

"Thank you, Frederick. Mr Aldridge will arrive soon for rehearsals, and tomorrow, the tenth of April, will be our opening night."

So the theatre isn't going to close after all! We will all keep our jobs. I'm excited and start to rush off-stage to find Trooper.

"Frederick!" Mr Simpkin's voice stops me. "Fetch me an early lunch. Today is going to be extremely busy." And he throws me a tuppence, which I catch in my left hand.

I walk into the wings. This is the space on both sides of the stage that the audience can't see. It's where the actors wait to "tread the boards", which means go on stage. It's also where the props table is and where the stage manager gives his signals from to make sure the show runs smoothly.

This is where Trooper is often found, curled up in a coil of rope. And here he is, as usual. I stop and take a morsel of fish out of my pocket, which I saved for him from this morning's breakfast. I put it under

his nose, which twitches a few times before he opens his eyes. He slowly gets up and stretches his back to make an arch; his front legs go straight as his body leans back; and then his back ones stretch out as his body leans forwards. Only then does he inspect the fish titbit, nibble it daintily, turn around in a full circle and lie down again in the coil of rope. He shuts his eyes and purrs loudly.

I give him a stroke and whisper in his ear.

"Trooper, we're going to have a real Othello tomorrow! Someone looking like me up on stage! I'm so excited!"

My next stop is the stage door on the ground floor. It makes me smile. The front of house, where the audience watch the play from, is always decked out in the latest fashion, with thick carpet on the stairs, mirrors and lights, but backstage is completely different. It's much more basic and there are definitely no frills or fancy decorations.

The wardrobe department is at the top of the stairs and less important actors have rooms off the stairs on different floors. These stairs never have any carpets and are bare stone.

"Where are you off to, Freddie my boy?" Benji, the stage doorman, asks me.

He's always there in his little cabin just inside the door, watching our comings and goings, dealing with tradesmen and protecting the theatre from anyone walking in off the street. I've noticed that if you're an actor, or someone important, everyone has to call you by your surname but, if you're like me or the stage doorman, everyone calls you by your first name.

"Off to buy Mr Simpkin's lunch," I say, skipping past.

"Bring me a quart of ale then," he says, flipping me a farthing, which I catch in my right hand this time.

I spend a lot of my time inside the theatre – it's my home and I love it a lot – but I do enjoy exploring the outside world as well. There's always so much to see on the streets of London!

CHAPTER FOUR

Once outside I breathe in deeply. The sun almost blinds me after the murky light inside the theatre. I have to squint my eyes. It feels warmer too, a proper spring day.

I love walking under the new colonnade, which runs along the side of the theatre, with its fluted columns and glass roof. The pillars go all along the whole side. I almost wish it was raining so I could watch the water pouring down from the sky and running off the roof, while I stay dry as I walk along underneath.

"Hello, Adeline," I say, stopping beside a young girl about my age selling posies of

violets, heather and lavender from a stall near the stage door. Her mother wheels her there every morning in her bath chair because she can't walk and collects her in the afternoon. Her mother works on a larger flower stall inside Covent Garden.

Sometimes, on my day off, I wheel Adeline up to Piccadilly where we look in the shop windows. We get stared at quite a lot, I think partly because Adeline is in her chair and partly because she is so beautiful with her long neck and shiny black hair.

Sometimes we go down Strand and look in the printing shop windows with their maps of the world. And there are bookshops too. One of them even has gas lighting, like we do in the theatre! And there are always lots of gentlemen lounging about in the coffee houses discussing the news and business.

Adeline's bath chair has a handle that connects to the front wheel so she can steer herself. This helps me to push it. I try not to go too fast if there are lots of people in case we bump into anyone.

Sometimes I walk along the river to the docks, especially the West India Quay where they unload sugar and rum from the West Indies, but I never take Adeline with me then. It's about four or five miles and, apart from it being too difficult to push the bath chair all that way, I don't think the sailors' language would be suitable for her ears. It's not really suitable for mine either! But I love to hear the stories they tell about far-off islands – what they look like and what is happening in them. I find you can learn a lot just by listening and watching.

Some of our stagehands used to be sailors. It was a surprise to me too but not after I thought about it. You see, sailors use a lot of ropes to hoist the canvas sails up and down and, in the theatre, most of the scenery is painted on canvas and is hoisted up and down on ropes. This is called "flying" the scenery – "in" when it's needed and "out" when the scene changes. That's why theatres are tall buildings, because that's where a lot of scenery is kept: up in the "flies" above the stage.

Both sailors and stagehands need to know how to knot the ropes off properly so everything is secure. And that makes me think of another thing. All these ropes for scenery and lights is called the "rigging", just like on a boat!

"Fred! Are you daydreaming again?"

It's Adeline, bringing me back to the present.

"You'll never guess what," I say, leaning

against the warm bricks of the wall.

"What?" Adeline replies.

"Ira Aldridge is coming to the theatre today."

"Who's he?"

"He's an actor. He's going to play Othello. We're making history."

Adeline doesn't look very interested as she continues twining a long piece of ribbon around some violets.

"He's black, like you and me."

Adeline stops what she's doing and looks at me. "An African actor? I've never heard of one before."

"I think he's American. He's played in other cities. He's quite famous actually."

"Well, I hope he's nice. Maybe he'll want to buy a posy for his missus."

"Maybe he will, Adeline. I'll tell him you're here. Got to go − I'm on an errand. Can I bring you anything?"

"No, I've got everything I need thanks, Fred. Bye!"

I set off, turn onto Brydges Street and cross the road. I always take a few moments to look at the front of the theatre and my heart bursts with pride every time, knowing that I work there. It's the oldest theatre in London. Well, not exactly this one, because the first building burned down. The second one got so old it was knocked down before it fell over. Then the third building also burned down because it had to use candles for lights and there was an accident.

This Theatre Royal is quite new, but it's still older than me. It looks grand with its columns and three large welcoming doors. I look up. It's very high, because of what I told you about flying the scenery. Let me see. The coal man says his horse is 15 hands (that's how grown-ups measure the height of horses) and the theatre is at least 20 horses high if you could stand them on top of each other like acrobats. So that would be … how many hands?

I bite my lip and concentrate. I use my fingers to help me count. But in the end I give up. A lot of hands I decide, setting off along the cobbled streets towards Covent Garden.

I'll buy the quart of ale for Benji on the way back, from The Lamb, the pub opposite the theatre. I'll need to get Mr Simpkin's madeira wine there too. I know what Mr Simpkin wants for his lunch – he doesn't need to tell me because it's always the same. He likes an oyster pie, washed down with a beef and broth soup.

I love the smell of the street. It's of horses and hay and street food. A fresh breeze is blowing off the Thames, bringing the sound of boats clacking together and voices riding on the wind. Horses' hooves clop, their harnesses jangle and people have to raise their voices to be heard. It's a din, a right old London din, and I love it.

Here I am now, in Covent Garden. It's brand new. The builders have almost all gone; there are just one or two left, putting the finishing touches to the outside.

It's taken them three years to strip out the tumble-down Hungerford Market and Covent Garden now looks like one of our stage sets. I could be in Venice or Verona, with the big open square and the market under the rows of pillars.

I mingle with the bustling crowds of shoppers and stallholders, pretending I'm one of the "Two Gentlemen of Verona" that Shakespeare wrote about. We had that play in the theatre last year.

Newspaper sellers are always shouting out the latest news, hoping to sell their papers to the passers-by. Normally I don't take much notice but sometimes the shouts catch my attention. The other day I learned that the Factory Act is going to become law soon. That means children younger than nine years old won't be allowed to work in factories any more.

I'm pleased about that because small children have to creep into the weaving machines to clean them. The machines don't stop, so the children have to pick up bits of fluff as the machine whizzes around. I feel sorry for those children because it's dangerous work and they can get hurt.

Older children like me will only have to work nine hours and even older children won't be allowed to work more than twelve hours. That's good, because at the moment many children have to get up and go to work when it's still dark in the morning. Sometimes they won't finish until night-time so in winter they don't see the sun at all.

I'm lucky because my work pattern means I don't have to get up too early. That's because I work evenings instead, six a week. We finish work late after the shows but we don't put the scenery back until the following day, and once we've done that we get a break until the next performance.

Right now the newspaper sellers are shouting out something that makes me stop and listen. Mr Simpkin is going to have to wait a little longer for his lunch.

"Parliament to pass Slavery Abolition Act!"

"Slavery soon over in the British colonies!"

This is important news. I feel excited. When I was down at the West India Quay just after Christmas, I heard the sailors talking about an enslaved man in Jamaica called Sam Sharpe who led a rebellion so men and women could get paid for the work they did. They didn't win, but everyone realized that freedom was coming whether the slave masters liked it or not.

There's a place in London called Parliament, Mrs Booth says, that makes laws for the future in Britain and the Empire. A politician called Mr William Wilberforce has been trying for years to make the other members of parliament pass a law to free all of the enslaved people. The King didn't want to free anyone and neither did his friends, but it looks as if the kind and generous Queen got her way on both matters.

Mr Wilberforce is finally going to get his bill through Parliament. I'm glad. It's not fair when people work for nothing. Hurrah!

CHAPTER FIVE

"Wretched cat!"

Mr Simpkin has a rolled-up newspaper in his hand, swiping it at the waste-paper basket, which falls over. Three mice jump

out and scatter as the basket comes to a halt sideways on the floor.

"Lazy little blighter! He's good for nothing that Trooper. Put my lunch on the table, Frederick, and go and make sure there are no mice to be seen in Mr Aldridge's dressing room."

"Yes, Mr Simpkin."

Mr Simpkin's office is on the ground floor, near the stage door. I make my way down the stairs to the stage level where the important dressing rooms are.

I'm looking forward to meeting Mr Aldridge.

As always, I knock before entering a dressing room. I find Mrs Booth already there so I know any mice will be hiding until the coast is clear. I need to remember to tell Trooper to pull his breeches up.

"Hello, Fred. We're expecting the African

Roscius any time now."

"What does 'Rosky-oos' mean, Mrs Booth?"

"Don't ask me," she says. "I just know that's his nickname."

She goes behind the screen, where the actors change into their costumes, and comes out again with some jackets and waistcoats over her arm. She plops them onto the couch and picks one up.

"Hold this jacket up against you, will you."

Mrs Booth hands me a jacket made of silk.

"Better still, slip it on for me quickly."

I wipe my hands on my overalls and take the jacket. It feels smooth. Mrs Booth helps me into it and hands me a tie to match. I can't help looking in the mirror and hardly recognize myself. I look fantastic – so handsome with my dark brown skin, corkscrew black curls and a cheeky smile.

I stand to attention, make a salute and give myself a wink.

"Just as I thought," says Mrs Booth, and a crease appears between her eyebrows. "It's only a little bit too large for you. Mr Aldridge is much bigger than Mr Kean."

She has one hand folded across her chest and the other is pulling at her chin.

"Oh dearie, dearie me! I shall be up all night and day stitching new costumes. Not to mention the cost. Mr Simpkin isn't going to like this at all."

I take the jacket off and lay it on the couch.

Just as I am deciding what to say to help Mrs Booth feel better, the door opens and Mr Ira Aldridge, the African "*Rosky-oos*" himself, fills up the doorway. He beams at us and moves forward.

I can see straight away that he is much taller than me, much taller in fact than anyone I know. He is also much younger than I imagined. He fills up the room. He's got hair like mine, but so much neater!

He's wearing a dark brown tailcoat of wool broadcloth with a velvet collar that fits

him perfectly. His waistcoat is black silk and his trousers plain cotton twill. His neck cloth is a dark plum colour and is tied loosely around his neck. He looks very smart.

Mr Simpkin follows him into the room and introduces Mrs Booth. Ira Aldridge bows and takes her hand.

"Enchanted to meet you," he says.

Mrs Booth drops a quick curtsy and blushes.

I feel quite shy, but his voice fills me with confidence. Mr Aldridge is very charming, with his strong American accent.

"And this is Frederick," Mr Simpkin says. "If you want anything, just ask him to fetch it for you."

Ira Aldridge turns to me and bows.

"Pleased to meet you, Frederick. I shall remember your name. It's my middle name, you see. Ira Frederick Aldridge, at your service."

"Pleased to meet you, Mr Aldridge," I say, bowing in return. He is so formal! "Everyone calls me Fred. Well, nearly everyone," I say, looking at Mr Simpkin.

"And so will I," he says, winking at me, before looking around the room.

Mrs Booth has tried to tidy it up but I can see it's still grubby. The screen is stained and the walls have dirty marks on them. The paint has yellowed with age and is peeling off in places.

Mr Simpkin clears his throat to get our attention back.

"I see you've been looking at the costumes, Mrs Booth," he says, spying the jacket. "Excellent. That one will do splendidly, I'm sure."

"It will not fit Mr Aldridge. He is a bigger man than Mr Kean," Mrs Booth says.

"I'm sure all that's needed is to move a few buttons. I've no doubt all the costumes can be made to fit." Mr Simpkin stares at Mrs Booth, who looks helplessly back at him. There is a silence before Mrs Booth finds her voice.

"It will not fit. It barely fits the boy. See this waistcoat?" She holds up a beautifully quilted dark green velvet waistcoat with gilt buttons. "It will not fit Mr Aldridge either."

Mr Aldridge swiftly removes his coat and waistcoat. He squeezes into the dark green velvet and does up the buttons. He takes a deep breath and, instantly, a button pops off. I catch it before it hits Mr Simpkin in the head!

There is another silence.

"Nothing will fit. And I am sure," Mrs Booth now stares at Mr Simpkin, "there will not be time to make a whole new wardrobe by tomorrow evening." She is close to tears.

"If I may?" Mr Aldridge has taken off the waistcoat and is putting his own back on. "I suggest that only one new outfit is made. Wardrobe must have cloaks and neck cloths that can be made use of to ring the changes. This will solve all the problems. Mrs Booth will not be overworked and the theatre need not be put to undue expense. What do you say?"

Mrs Booth and Mr Aldridge look at Mr Simpkin who, after a moment's hesitation, agrees.

"That is very gracious of you, Mr Aldridge. Mrs Booth, please take measurements and proceed. Frederick, come with me."

CHAPTER SIX

I'm in the wardrobe department, my favourite place in the theatre, with Trooper and Mrs Booth. Mrs Booth is sorting through some neck cloths ready for pressing and has some little flat irons resting on a coal pot. Although they are little they're heavy because, you've guessed it, they are made of iron! She picks one up by its wooden handle to test how hot it is. She runs the iron over a piece of brown paper and checks to see if it has made any scorch marks.

I'm finishing off a bowl of Mrs Booth's very fine vegetable soup. I have to take my lunch break later than everyone else in case they need anything. Once they are all busy rehearsing again then I have some free time.

"Thank you, Mrs Booth, that was tasty," I say.

"Thank you, Fred," she says. "I'm glad you like my soup, but don't you mean delicious, dearie? I want you to practise interesting words."

"*Di-li-shus*. But it was tasty all the same. Why do you want me to practise interesting words?"

I put my soup bowl on the floor and Trooper, who has been waiting patiently at my feet, staring at me with his green eyes opening and shutting, hunches over it. I watch him lick it clean before breaking off a small piece of bread and dropping it on the floor for him.

"Well, Freddie dear," she says, "I just think you will sound more ... interesting."

She makes me laugh sometimes.

I see a book on her workbench.

"What are you reading?" I ask her. She reads a lot, quite slowly, and has to move her mouth as she forms the words. She's teaching me to read as well.

"I won't be reading much today. Or tomorrow," she says. "This one's called *Frankenstein* and it's scaring me."

"Why, what's it about?"

"It's about a clever scientist who makes a monster that only eats vegetables and gets lonely. A young lady wrote it. Why don't you read out her name, Fred?"

I pick the book up and look at the cover.

"*Frankenstein*," I say, feeling proud. It's a long word to read but I remember what Mrs Booth said.

I look at the next word. "By Mary," I say. I know that one because it's Mrs Booth's name and we practise writing out our names sometimes.

"Sh-Sh-Sh—" I know those two letters together sound different to when they're on their own. "Shell—"

"Yes, that's right, dear, it starts just as in Shakespeare."

"Shelley?"

"Well done, Fred!" Mrs Booth says. "Her name is Mary Shelley and not so long ago she brought out a new edition, so I thought I'd try it. *Frankenstein* made her famous and she's still only a young woman."

A lonely monster that only eats vegetables doesn't sound very scary to me so I don't say anything more. I put the book down and decided to ask her something that's been playing on my mind all day.

"Mrs Booth, when I went into the pub earlier I heard some of the stagehands talking.

They were saying horrible things about Mr Aldridge."

"Like what, dear?"

"They were saying it's a disgrace he's being allowed to play Othello, and all because he isn't white like them."

"You don't want to pay attention to everything you hear, Freddie. Some people hate things, and people, that are different from what they're used to."

I understand that because I've heard people make fun of me when I pass by, being rude about my hair and the colour of my skin. It still hurts my feelings but I try not to take any notice. I mean, why don't people like me? I'm very polite and kind, I work hard and everyone who knows me likes me. It upsets me that people can be so mean sometimes.

"Look at your mother, for instance."

I don't move. I love it when Mrs Booth talks about my mother. I don't want anything to stop her.

"Everyone said Mr Booth shouldn't take her on, and only because she looked a bit different from them. They didn't even know her."

Mrs Booth picks up another neck cloth to iron. I wait to see if she will say anything else but she's busy flicking water on it with her fingers.

"What else, Mrs Booth?"

"What do you want to hear, Fred?"

"What she was like."

"Well, Dora was a wonderful seamstress. Mr Booth never had to tell her anything twice; she always knew what to do and when to do it. And her stitches were always strong and neat."

Mrs Booth has done two neck cloths

already. She puts the iron back on the coal pot before picking up another of the irons, checking so it doesn't leave scorch marks, and carrying on.

"She was very clever too. She used to do all Mr Booth's accounts. She had a kind heart and loved animals. Why, Fred, I think you have taken after her."

"What about my father?"

"I can't tell you about your father, Fred, because I never knew him, but your mother always spoke very well of him. He was a soldier in the King's Army and died when you were a baby."

I'm sad about that. I would really like to know about my father. I hear the hiss of steam as Mrs Booth sprinkles another neck cloth with water before gliding an iron over it and putting it with the others. It doesn't look like she is going to say anything more.

"Have you any more water, Mrs Booth? I need to wash my handkerchief. It got used up last night."

She gives me a quick look.

"Over by the window, dearie. I'll press it for you later. When you've finished that I need you to take these neck cloths down to Mr Aldridge so he can choose four. And make sure you bring the rest back."

"Yes, Mrs Booth."

As soon as I've finished washing and rinsing out my handkerchief I hang it up and go back down to the dressing rooms.

No one is in Mr Aldridge's dressing room so I leave the neck cloths on the couch. He must be onstage.

I sneak into the darkened stalls quietly and sit next to Mr Simpkin, where he is conducting rehearsals. Sometimes the actors do the same bits over and over again.

They want to make sure they get the lines right and that they remember everything. Some stagehands find the endless going over everything boring, but I love seeing all the details taking shape. It's a lesson on how to become good at what you set your mind to.

There is only one working light on the stage, not like in a full performance when all the lamps are burning. It gets really hot when they are all lit up so it's more comfortable when they're off, and besides, Mr Simpkin is not going to waste any money if he can avoid it.

Even without the lights I can't take my eyes off Mr Aldridge. He really believes what he's saying and so he's making me believe it too. It's the scene with Miss Ellen Tree, who plays Desdemona, after she's lost the handkerchief Othello gave to her.

All of a sudden Othello hits her. I let out

a gasp as she falls down – it looks so real. But the next minute Mr Aldridge is helping her up, asking her if she is all right. They stop acting and, standing side by side, look into the stalls to hear what Mr Simpkin has to say.

"Indeed, it seems real enough." Mr Simpkin sounds embarrassed. I have never known him to be embarrassed. But I know why. "I am not sure, though, if it is … appropriate."

"Othello strikes Desdemona, does he not?" It is Miss Tree's question.

"Yes, b–but," Mr Simpkin stammers.

"You mean it has been appropriate up until now for Othello to hit Desdemona, but suddenly it has become inappropriate?"

"Well, um…" I can tell Mr Simpkin is searching for something to say.

"The answer is yes, is it not?" This time it is Mr Aldridge who speaks. He doesn't raise his voice, he doesn't sound angry, just strong.

I look sideways at Mr Simpkin. He has gone red.

"Yes," he says. There is a silence. "Only I am not sure how the audience will respond."

"Since I am *not* actually being hit, and Shakespeare himself has written it into the story, I believe we should do as he intended,"

Miss Tree says firmly.

"No man should ever hit a woman," Mr Aldridge says. "And to see it done on the stage is shocking, I agree. But it is meant to shock. We actors hold a mirror up to people and ask them to reflect on what they might themselves do."

Miss Tree nods her head in agreement. Mr Simpkin is silent.

I know what no one is saying. When both actors are white, the audience accepts the story, as they have always done. But now Mr Aldridge is playing Othello, it's suddenly different.

It has to do with some white people thinking they are better than black people because of the colour of their skin. This makes some of them treat us very differently to how they expect to be treated themselves. They say horrible things, beat us and treat us badly just because our skin is a different colour.

People believe what they're told by the newspapers or their parents. It takes a strong person to make their own mind up about someone who looks even a tiny bit different. As Mrs Booth said, people are afraid if something or someone is different from what they're used to. I am only nine and I can see that this is a foolish way to think. Surely, it's the way each of us behaves that makes us good people or not.

Mr Simpkin has been examining his copy of *Othello*. Suddenly he shuts the book and stands up.

"You are right," he says. "It is in the play and we shall do it. The audience will have to decide for themselves."

He pauses a moment before continuing.

"Rehearsals are over for the day.

Please stay until you know the call time for tomorrow. I will send Frederick to let you know."

I have a new feeling towards Mr Simpkin. I feel proud of him.

CHAPTER SEVEN

"Come in."

Mr Aldridge is reaching for his overcoat, getting ready to go home. He looks tired, but still has a smile for me.

"Hello, Fred," he says. "What time tomorrow?"

"Ten o'clock in the morning. And Mrs Booth sent those neck cloths down for you to choose. She says you can have four."

"Does she now?" Mr Aldridge drapes his coat on a chair. "I always find choosing difficult, Fred." He puts his head on one side as he looks them over. "Why don't you help me?"

"Me?" I say.

"Why not?"

I step over to the couch, feeling important.

"I think the green one, and this plain red one. You should have a white one and … um … this dark blue one?" I look up at him shyly.

"Done. Thank you, Fred, you made it much easier."

"Mr Aldridge?"

"Yes, Fred?"

"Why do they call you the African *Rosky-oos*?"

"Aha! Where did you hear that?"

I don't want to get anyone in trouble, just in case it meant something bad, so I tell him that I saw it on the playbill outside.

"Well, Fred, I'll tell you. I first played Othello here in London about eight years ago and a critic called me the African Roscius. They like to think they're clever, those critics. He was being sarcastic and wanted to insult me. You see, Quintus Roscius Gallus, to give him his full name, was a Roman actor and a former slave who taught Cicero."

"Who's Cicero?"

"He was a famous Roman writer. Have you heard the motto 'Where there's life, there's hope'?"

"Mr Simpkin always says it just before the curtain goes up on opening night."

"Well, he's quoting Cicero."

Mr Simpkin is full of surprises today. I didn't know he knew Romans.

"If someone compares an actor to Roscius it means you are very good, but this critic decided to call me the *African* Roscius as an insult. So I thought I would turn it round on him. I made it into my title and I use it all the time now. It works very well. Funny really."

I smile, feeling pleased Mr Aldridge got the better of a hoity-toity critic.

"You've got to remember, Fred, just because a person says something about you, that doesn't make it true. There are going to be people who won't like seeing me on stage doing Shakespeare, or anything else for that matter. But I'm not going to let that stop me. Meanwhile, we just have to be who we are. 'To thine own self be true.'"

"I know that one – we had *Hamlet* here a few times. Only, I'm not sure what it really means."

"It means have the courage to be yourself. It's a good motto for us all."

Mr Aldridge picks up his coat and puts his arm in a sleeve. I help him with the other one.

"You know, Fred, you have a lot to offer your friends and the world," Mr Aldridge says as he does up his coat.

"But I'm just a boy, Mr Aldridge, an orphan. I don't have anything to offer."

"You need to think about that," he says, reaching for his scarf and putting it around his neck. "We all have something, Fred. Whoever we are, wherever we come from, we all have something that can make a

difference."

I think about this and hope what he says is true. He stands in front of the long mirror and tucks his scarf into his coat. There is a faraway look in his eyes.

"I had to work during my boat journey to England. I was seventeen," he says.

I'm surprised. "What did you do?"

"I was a ship's steward." He must have seen my confusion because then he said, "That means being a waiter. I waited on tables."

He seems so grand. I can't imagine that once upon a time he was taking orders and carrying dirty plates to the kitchen on board a ship.

"Where were you born?" I ask.

"I was born in America and I'm guessing you were born in London."

"Yes," I say.

"We come from different parts of the

world but we share the same African heritage."

He sits down, as if he is going to tell me a story, so I sit back down too.

"Africa is a very large continent, you know, with ancient universities, music, architecture, whole civilizations. But people have been kidnapping its citizens for hundreds of years, taking them away from their families and selling them in distant places."

I remember the newspaper sellers I saw when I went out at lunchtime, shouting out the headlines. That very soon all the enslaved people in the British colonies are going to be set free.

"Mr Aldridge?"

"Yes, Fred?"

"Were you a slave? Did you run away?"

"No – my father was a preacher and we were born as free people in New York. They sent me to the African Free School in the city. But we always had to be careful because, even in New York, gangs would still try to kidnap people like us to sell into slavery."

I try to imagine what that must feel like, to live in fear of being taken away from your home and everyone you love.

"Do you know, when I was young I watched Shakespeare plays just like you do."

"Really?"

"Yes, but the shows were performed in the park. Can you imagine? There I was, a young black boy in New York, watching William Shakespeare's plays in a park! And the funny thing is, I really enjoyed them. They spoke to me. And then a company of black actors began performing Shakespeare."

"Really?" I said again. I can't imagine that happening in London.

"Everyone I knew enjoyed the shows,

but the company didn't last long. It was closed down because so many white people objected. I wondered why white people couldn't see what we saw – that emotions don't just affect certain people. We all have feelings, no matter our race. Or age, for that matter."

He is talking to me like a grown-up, telling me about when he was a boy, and not just giving me orders or teaching me. Mr Aldridge doesn't look down on me like some people do. He is talking to me with respect and I feel as if he understands me.

"I mean to say," he carries on, "how old is fear? Do you think it has a birthday?"

I laugh. The idea is funny. It makes him laugh too.

"And what about love? Don't we all share that feeling?"

I nod my head, thinking about all the

feelings I have and the people I care about.

"Do you think only Englishmen love and only Americans fear?"

"Now you're being silly," I say, and we laugh some more.

"Anyway, I knew that when I grew up I wanted to be an actor. I got quite well known but ... well, there weren't many parts in New York for people of colour. So I thought I'd tread the boards over here."

I'm wondering how old he is. He's certainly not as old as Mr Simpkin. I could just ask him, only that wouldn't be very polite. But I can see he is someone who isn't afraid to try very hard to make his dreams come true.

"Like I said, 'To thine own self be true', Fred. Discover what you're good at and learn how to do it really well."

He gets up, walks over to the door and

opens it.

"And now, young man," he says, "we have a long day tomorrow. It's our opening night! I'd better go home and get some sleep. And so should you."

"Yes, Mr Aldridge. Goodnight."

"Goodnight, Fred." And Mr Aldridge closes the door behind him.

I put the four neck cloths onto a coat hanger and pick up the remaining ones, before stepping out.

The theatre is very quiet now. I'm about to go up to the wardrobe department but change my mind and walk onto the stage instead.

There is always one light left on, right in the middle of the stage. It's called the ghost light and is not very bright.

Every theatre is supposed to have at least one ghost. I've never seen one so I'm

not sure that it's true. It's another theatre superstition. One light is left burning so the ghost can feel at home and perform, if it wants to.

Personally, I think the light is left on so you don't fall over anything in the dark. For instance, if a trapdoor was left open it would be horrible to fall down into one. That reminds me to have a proper look around as I pick my way on to the stage.

I find the middle of the heavy curtain that separates the stage from all the empty seats and slide through the opening. I look out into the auditorium. It's pitch black, and I feel as if I'm looking into my future. Who knows what it will really be like?

My daydreams help me to imagine different futures but I will need to choose one of my very own. To thine own self be true, he said. Discover what I'm good at. Make a difference.

Mr Aldridge has given me a lot to think about.

CHAPTER EIGHT

Later, after I've shared my supper with Trooper, we curl up in my cosy corner. I love it in there. My own space where I can dream and think and be myself.

I wonder what Mr Aldridge must be feeling right now, if he's nervous or not. He has so many lines to learn and then he has to remember them all once he goes on stage in front of all those people. My heart gives a little flutter just thinking about it and it isn't even me that has to do it. You've got to be very brave to be an actor.

My eyes start to close. I feel very tired all of a sudden.

I wake up in the morning to Trooper sniffing my face. I stretch and start stroking his back.

"Oh, Trooper, I dreamt I had to play Othello last night and I didn't know the words! I began to make them up and the whole audience started laughing. Then the actors set off laughing too and a long line of mice raced onstage, being chased by you. The audience started clapping. You looked surprised but stopped and took a bow."

Trooper just purrs loudly and paws my chest. He jumps off lightly when I push the blanket off and brushes against my legs while I get dressed.

Then I take the supper leftovers out of the cupboard and pour a saucer of milk out before putting them down for Trooper, who mews a thank you. It's a big day today.

After I've swept the stage I go and get

Mr Simpkin. He inspects my work, moves to one side and gives a low whistle. The stagehands start to lower the painted canvas flats down onto the bare stage and once again we are in a street in Venice.

I follow Mr Simpkin offstage where we see Trooper fast asleep in his usual spot. Mr Simpkin stops and looks at him thoughtfully.

"What is it, Mr Simpkin?" I say.

"That cat has got to go."

I'm taken aback. "Why is that, Mr Simpkin?"

"He's not doing his job – he never catches mice any more. I can't afford any slackers. Look at him, lying there, while we run around working hard. You hear that, Trooper my lad, you're fired! I'm on the lookout for a new cat." And he stalks into his office and slams the door.

I can't help it – my bottom lip starts to quiver and tears spring up. I wipe them away with my sleeve. Just then, Mr Aldridge passes by on his way to the stage.

"Why, Fred, whatever's the matter?"

"Nothing," I say.

"Something has upset you. Come into my dressing room and tell me what's happened."

He turns around and leads the way back to his dressing room and I follow him. He sits on his chair and waits.

I start to tell him what Mr Simpkin said about Trooper. It's difficult because I have to stop and take deep breaths. But he listens patiently until I finish.

"I see," he says. "Why do you think Trooper has stopped catching mice, Fred?"

"I don't know," I say, feeling like crying all over again. "He's my best friend. I don't want to lose him."

An image comes into my mind of me sharing my breakfast fish with Trooper yesterday. And then I remember the saucers of milk I give him every morning.

"What is it, Fred?"

"Nothing," I say again, but this time I have an idea.

"You look like you were thinking about something."

"Well… I love Trooper, he's my best friend and so I always give him little snacks."

"I see," Mr Aldridge says. Then he adds, "Remember yesterday when we were talking about making a difference?"

"Yes."

"Well, sometimes you make a difference by doing something, but sometimes you make a difference by not doing something. Does that make sense?"

I look at him.

"Yes, Mr Aldridge, it does," I say.

"Off you go then, Fred. I need to go onstage and do my warm-ups."

I stand at the door.

"Thank you, Mr Aldridge, and – and I know I shouldn't say it…"

"No, don't, Fred, but thanks."

I wanted to wish him the very best of luck tonight. But the theatre is a funny place with lots of superstitions. It's bad luck to wish anyone good luck! And black cats are supposed to be unlucky, but in the theatre they bring good luck! I wonder if there are other workplaces where things seem back to front, inside out or upside down?

I spend the rest of the day doing my jobs and now it's early evening. I'm sitting in the wardrobe department with Mrs Booth.

I've been scampering up and down the stairs announcing the "Half", which means it's thirty minutes until the show starts, and the moment when all the actors have to be in their dressing rooms.

Then I have to go around and say, "Quarter of an hour, ladies and gentlemen; you have fifteen minutes."

Then I say, "Five," and, finally, "Beginners, please." For that call, I only knock on the doors of the actors who begin the show. Then, during the show, I have to knock to let each actor know when to make their way down to the stage in time for their cue. This means I get to know everyone and everyone gets to know me. It's a busy time for me as I have to keep looking at the clock and stay focused.

Mrs Booth is taking a breather. She stitched all night back at her house. She's lucky because Mr Booth is a tailor and able to help make the costume for Mr Aldridge. It fits beautifully and she is feeling triumphant but tired.

She's given me a dry biscuit to keep me going and Trooper is curling around my feet again. I break off a piece of biscuit and then remember I mustn't give him any. Not if I want him to stay. He changes tactic, mews and looks at me steadily, opening and

shutting his eyes, hoping, I suppose, that I will take pity on him. I do feel sorry for him but keep my promise to myself and don't feed him. He jumps onto my lap and starts sniffing the biscuit, which I have to hold away from him.

"I know," I say. "I know you'd like some. And you are still my best friend but I mustn't feed you any more in case you lose your job." And I push him off my lap.

"Do you think Trooper will still like me if I don't feed him any morsels?"

Mrs Booth gives a jump. "What's that, dearie?"

"Sorry, I didn't realize you were sleeping. I said do you think Trooper will still want to be my friend if I don't feed him any more?"

"Of course he will, Freddie. Friendship is about more than food. It's about caring."

Trooper is still looking at me. I'm not

sure he understands, but I do. I look at the clock again.

"I've got to go down now and call the 'Five'. I'll stay down for 'Beginners' so I'll see you in a while, Mrs Booth."

"Before you go, Fred." Mrs Booth gets up from her comfy chair. "Here is your handkerchief, all pressed."

She picks it up from the ironing table and hands it to me. She is such a kind lady and she knows how much my mother's handkerchief means to me. I fold it carefully and put it in my trouser pocket so it stays neat.

After I've done the rounds I take up my post next to Mr Simpkin in the wings. I can hear the audience. There are lots of people out there. An excited babble of voices gives my stomach a sudden flip. I peep through a tiny hole in one of the curtains and see lots of ladies and gentlemen settling into their seats.

The enormous chandelier pulled up high in the middle of the stalls is like an upside-down umbrella, shedding light from every part. The jewels from the ladies in the audience reflect the light and make patterns on the walls of the theatre.

It's like looking at a different world. Everyone is wearing their best clothes – there are so many colours and fabrics and jewels and accessories. I play a game with myself to spot the person in the fanciest outfit. I spy a lady sitting in the stalls. Her apricot-coloured evening gown shows her neck and shoulders; the short sleeves puff out, stopping above her elbow. Her arm is raised and she is looking through her opera glasses. My eyes follow to where she is looking and a gentleman from across the stalls bows in her direction. She removes the opera glasses and waves at him. She settles back in her red velvet cushioned seat and looks towards the stage.

Good luck, Mr Aldridge; good luck, everyone, I say silently in my head.

Mr Simpkin has checked the stage to make sure everything is ready for the performance and the two actors who open the show are present. He is waiting for an usher to come through the pass door that connects the front of house to the backstage. Once the usher comes to tell him all the audience are in their seats he then gives the order to raise the curtain.

As soon as that happens I know Mr Simpkin will check his pocket watch, and when he closes it he will rub it in a circle three times one way and then three times the other before putting it back. He does

this every night. It's more than a habit;
it's a ritual, to make sure the show goes well.

Everyone has their own ritual. I always put
my hand in my pocket and feel for the "D"

embroidered on my mother's handkerchief. I squeeze it hard between my thumb and forefinger. I wonder what our new Othello's ritual is before he steps on to the stage.

There is a hush backstage – everyone is concentrating on what they have to do for the next two hours. That's one of the things I love about the theatre. Each and every one of us plays an important part of the whole. We achieve together. It's a team effort.

The usher comes through the pass door and nods at Mr Simpkin.

"Where there's life, there's hope," Mr Simpkin mutters, pulling out his pocket watch.

Then he gives a short whistle and I help pull on the rope to raise the curtain. The lights go down in the audience and come up bright on stage. We're off!

CHAPTER NINE

Mr Aldridge and all the cast are wonderful. My heart is bursting with pride, seeing the actors playing their parts, the scenery flying in and out on low whistled orders, taking us first to Venice and then to Cyprus. (That's why its unlucky to whistle in a theatre, because a piece of scenery might fly down and knock you over.)

I heard some stagehands whispering that Ira Aldridge is much better than they ever expected. Of course he is – he's my hero. My thunder roll was perfect too, even if I say so myself!

We've got to the first interval. I knock

on Mr Aldridge's dressing-room door with a pitcher of cordial and walk in, ready to congratulate him.

Mr Simpkin is in there with him, along with Mrs Booth. Something is not right. They all look very worried.

Mr Simpkin is saying, "Mine blew away this morning on my way into work. I took it out to blow my nose and the wind

whipped it out of my hand and cast it into the sky. I dare say it's still blowing down the Thames. It might have reached the North Sea by now." His voice is getting higher. "I can't understand it," he continues. "Has there been a proper search? How is it lost? It can't just have disappeared. It must be here somewhere."

Mrs Booth is wringing her hands. "Oh dear, oh dearie me, mine are all in the boiling pot. There isn't a single one up in the wardrobe department that isn't dripping wet. Whatever shall we do? We need one right away. There's so little time."

"Frederick'," Mr Simpkin says. "Go up to Benji at the stage door and collect his handkerchief. It doesn't matter what state it's in, get it off him."

I do immediately as he says, crossing my fingers all the way that Benji has a handkerchief. I listen to Benji's story and race back to the dressing room with the news.

"Benji threw his away this morning. He cut his finger and stopped the blood with it. He decided he couldn't ever use it again and threw it on the fire."

Everyone stands there not knowing what to do. Desdemona's handkerchief is the proof that makes Othello believe Iago's lies. I bite my lip.

"Please, Mr Simpkin," I say, putting my hand in my pocket and bringing out my most precious treasure. "You can use mine."

"But that's your mother's, Freddie." Mrs Booth turns to Mr Simpkin. "It's Dora's. It's all that he has to remember her by. Surely we can find one handkerchief in the whole of the theatre?"

I look at Mrs Booth. "There isn't time,"

I say. "Honestly, it's all right, Mr Simpkin, you can use it."

I hold it out to him.

Mr Simpkin looks me in the eye. "Thank you, Fred," he says. He takes it with a sigh of relief. "I shan't forget this."

Mr Aldridge doesn't say anything but looks at me seriously.

Mr Simpkin says, "I shall take it myself to Miss Tree right this minute and we shall bring the curtain up on time. Fred, you have saved the evening!"

I smile a wobbly smile.

CHAPTER TEN

It's early in the morning and I'm still under the blanket in my cosy corner. It's getting light much earlier now. There's blossom on the trees in Covent Garden and I can hear the sparrows on the rooftops but I don't feel very chirpy myself.

Trooper didn't curl up with me last night. I don't think he likes me any more and will soon forget me. I reach under my pillow for my mother's handkerchief and then remember I don't have it.

I'm pleased, of course, that I was able to help last night. Mr Aldridge is a wonderful man and he deserved for everything to be perfect. I know Mrs Booth will have another handkerchief for tonight but I hope they haven't lost mine like the other one. Then what will I do? I'll be all on my own in the world.

I hear Mrs Booth come in and move around. She doesn't talk to me as usual, or peep round the curtain to see if I'm all right. I expect she's busy. I listen. Soon she's gone and it's quiet again. Maybe she's forgotten about me too.

After I've swept the stage I decide to see if Trooper is in his usual spot, curled up asleep in the wings. He isn't. What if Mr Simpkin has already thrown him out? I didn't even get a chance to say goodbye or find out where he might have gone. My shoulders droop and I make my way slowly back up the stairs. Each step looks lonelier and sounds more hollow as I trudge up the stairs.

Once back in the wardrobe department I find it's empty again, although Mrs Booth has lit the coal pot and her irons are warming on the grid above it. I look in the cupboard and see she's left some bread and a glass of milk. I'm not sure if it's for me. It usually is. To be honest, I'm not hungry.

Mrs Booth comes in.

"Oh there you are, Fred. I've been looking for you. Mr Simpkin says you are to come down at once to Mr Aldridge's dressing room."

And she leaves quickly. I follow her down slowly.

I step inside. Mr Aldridge, Mr Simpkin and Mrs Booth are all in there and they watch me as I come in.

Mr Aldridge clears his throat.

"Desdemona's handkerchief has been found, Fred. We will never know if it went missing by accident, or if it was on purpose. It doesn't matter now. But what we do know is, you saved the show."

Then it's Mr Simpkin's turn.

"Fred, I know I don't always show how much I appreciate the hard work you put in. You're always on time and you never complain. Your quick thinking and kindness last night prevented a disaster. How would you like to change some of your jobs and work with me front of house as well?"

I don't know what to say. My clothes are so shabby and old compared to what people wear on that side of the curtain. I think I shall have to say no thank you very much, even though I want to say yes please.

But before I can say anything, Mrs Booth goes behind the screen and brings out a new jacket of dark green silk and a pale-yellow embroidered waistcoat. It's far too small for Mr Aldridge.

"I made this for you, Fred, to say thank you for last night. It was a difficult thing for you to do and I admire you for it. Now, try this on for size please."

I change out of my dirty overalls, which have gone all shiny in places from age, into a clean shirt and trousers. Mrs Booth bundles me into the new waistcoat. She makes me hold up my arms and puts me into the jacket. Mrs Booth looks at me and beams.

"It's perfect, Fred. Why, you look like the exceptional young man you are and it will be perfect for your new duties front of house. Take a look in the mirror."

"Thank you, Mrs Booth," I say, as I look at myself in the mirror and see her smiling down at me.

"Fred?" Mr Aldridge says.

I turn to him and he's holding up my handkerchief, all newly washed and pressed.

He bends down and puts it carefully in my pocket.

Then he stands up and says, "There. Safe and sound. Mrs Booth told us what that handkerchief means to you. Your mother would be proud. You made a difference, Fred, a big difference to the success of the show. Thank you."

Then he looks at Mrs Booth.

"And these are for you, Mrs Booth, to thank you for all your hard work over the last few days."

He picks up a posy of violets from a small table and gives them to her. They're from Adeline; I recognize the way she ties the ribbon. Mr Aldridge is the nicest man I've ever met.

I can hardly speak from happiness, but there is one thing that is making me sad. Where is my best friend?

"Has anyone seen Trooper? I haven't seen him since yesterday. Have you fired him,

Mr Simpkin?"

Mr Simpkin opens his mouth to reply and, right on cue, there is a kerfuffle from behind the screen. We all stop to listen. Trooper appears from behind it with a mouse in his jaws. He comes over to me and drops the mouse at my feet. I think this means he's forgiven me.

"Well, well, well, you just saved your bacon, Trooper my lad," Mr Simpkin says.

I start laughing and clapping and everyone else does too. Trooper picks up his mouse and disappears behind the screen again.

Ira Frederick Aldridge smiles at me and I, Fred Jonas, smile back.

"You really are an extraordinary young man, Fred, with a great future ahead of you. I can see it. Can you?" he says.

"Yes, Mr Aldridge," I say. "I think I can!"

HISTORICAL NOTE

London is already an old city when our story begins in 1833.

About 1,800 years before, the Romans built a bridge across the River Thames and then decided it would be a good place to build a city. Ships sailed up the River Thames from the sea, anchored there and unloaded their cargo. Like Rome, London attracted people from all over the world who made it their home.

Although our story is set in London, Ira Aldridge was born in New York, USA, in 1807. Just like Fred, Ira Aldridge grew up with a love for the theatre and the stage.

The African Grove Theatre in New York put on Shakespeare plays and Ira Aldridge started his apprenticeship at the theatre.

He first performed the part of Rolla in the play *Pizarro* by Richard Brinsley Sheridan in 1822, as well as Romeo in Shakespeare's *Romeo and Juliet*.

Ira Aldridge and Charles Kean, the son of the famous actor Edmund Kean, were friends at the time of our story and continued to be friends after, acting together many more times. And, by the way, Charles Kean and Ellen Tree, who played Iago and Desdemona, got married!

Sadly, Ira Aldridge performed as Othello at the Theatre Royal only twice before the show was cancelled. The London critics continued their racist behaviour and complained about him.

Ira Aldridge made his mind up not to work on the London stage again. He continued acting in shows up and down the country and was popular with his audiences.

A few years later Ira Aldridge toured in Europe where he played Othello again, to excellent reviews. He became friends with lots of important people, such as the King of Prussia and famous artists. Different countries awarded him medals and honours, including the Prussian Gold Medal of Arts and Sciences, the Golden Cross of Leopold from the Czar of Russia and the Maltese Cross from Switzerland.

When Ira Aldridge returned to London he was a famous, celebrated and rich man. This time, he chose which theatres he played in and what parts he played. Characters were rewritten for him and his earlier critics had to recognize his success.

Ira Aldridge was married twice. First to an English woman called Margaret Gill. A year after Margaret died in 1864, Ira Aldridge married again to a Swedish lady named Amanda von Brandt. Ira Aldridge had several children, including a daughter called Luranah who grew up to be a famous singer.

By the time Ira Aldridge died he was a famous actor in England, Europe and America, where a theatre company was formed in his name.

If you ever go to the Theatre Royal in London, look out for a bust of Ira Aldridge in the foyer.

The Theatre Royal is supposedly the most haunted theatre in Britain! The most famous ghost said to haunt the theatre is that of the actor Joseph Grimaldi, who invented the first "clown" face that we see in the circus today.

P.S. There really was a tailor called Mr Booth who lived and worked in Drury Lane around this time.

GLOSSARY

Act	The main sections of a play or a musical.
Applause	When the audience claps to show they enjoyed the performance.
Audience	The people watching a performance.
Backstage	The part of a theatre which is not seen by the audience, including the dressing rooms and the wings.
Balcony	The highest level of seats in a theatre, above the dress or upper circle.
Beginners	The actors who start the show.
Box office	The booth where theatre tickets are sold.
Call	The time an actor or crew has to be inside the theatre and ready for the performance.

Cast	The actors who perform in a show.
Crew	All the people who work the scenery and the lights, and make the costumes.
Critic	A person who comments on and recommends (or not) a play or show for people to see.
Cue	The part or line that happens just before an actor's turn on stage. Actors have to listen and watch for this so that they are prepared to have their turn at the right moment.
Dress circle	The first raised area of theatre seats for the audience.
Flats	Canvas stretched across a frame and painted with a scene to help the audience locate the action. These were often pulled up out of sight and so had to be light.
Flies	The area out of sight above the stage where scenery is stored during the play. It is flown in or out as required.

Foyer	A large entrance area where people can meet or wait inside the main doors of the theatre.
Front of house	The part of the theatre known as the auditorium where the audience is seated, and where the foyer and the box office are found.
Gallery	The top level in the theatre, where the audience can sometimes stand.
"Go dark"	A phrase to describe when a theatre closes if there is no performance or show.
Lines	The dialogue of the play. Each actor has to learn what they are going to say (their "part") for the performance.
Open the show	The start of the show. It is sometimes called the "top of the show".
Pass door	The door that connects the front of house to the backstage area.

Playbill	The poster that announces which show is going to performed at the theatre.
Programme	A printed booklet available for the audience attending a theatre performance, giving more information on the play and the actors.
Prompt copy	A prompt copy has all of the lines the actors say, as well as moves they make. It also has the scene changes and anything else to do with the production. It is a very important book.
Props	All the items used in a play to tell the story, not including the scenery or costumes.
Rehearsal	A session before the show opens when the actors practise their roles.
Rigging	The ropes that bring the scenery and lights down onto the stage and up again at the end of a scene.

Stagehand	A member of the theatre crew.
Stalls	The area where part of the audience sits to watch the play. It is usually slightly below the stage and slopes up away from the stage so the people at the back still have a good view.
"Tread the boards"	A phrase describing when the actors are on stage playing their part.
Upper circle	The level of seats in the theatre above the dress circle.
Usher	A man or woman who directs you to your seat, sells programmes and is trained to help in case of an emergency.
Warm-ups	Physical and vocal exercises actors do before the play starts, to make sure they are ready to perform.
Wings	The area around the stage that the audience can't see.